TRAVEL TO...

THE SCENE OF THE CRIME

Lisa Kurkov

T0014683

Rourke.

BEFORE AND DURING READING ACTIVITIES

Before Reading: *Building Background Knowledge and Vocabulary*

Building background knowledge can help children process new information and build upon what they already know. Before reading a book, it is important to tap into what children already know about the topic. This will help them develop their vocabulary and increase their reading comprehension.

Questions and Activities to Build Background Knowledge:

1. Look at the front cover of the book and read the title. What do you think this book will be about?
2. What do you already know about this topic?
3. Take a book walk and skim the pages. Look at the table of contents, photographs, captions, and bold words. Did these text features give you any information or predictions about what you will read in this book?

Vocabulary: *Vocabulary Is Key to Reading Comprehension*

Use the following directions to prompt a conversation about each word:

- Read the vocabulary words.
- What comes to mind when you see each word?
- What do you think each word means?

Vocabulary Words:
- accomplices
- alibi
- domestic terrorists
- embezzling
- extortion
- heist
- forger
- impostor
- notorious
- replicas
- treason
- wiretapping

During Reading: *Reading for Meaning and Understanding*

To achieve deep comprehension of a book, children are encouraged to use close reading strategies. During reading, it is important to have children stop and make connections. These connections result in deeper analysis and understanding of a book.

 Close Reading a Text

During reading, have children stop and talk about the following:

- Any confusing parts
- Any unknown words
- Text to text, text to self, text to world connections
- The main idea in each chapter or heading

Encourage children to use context clues to determine the meaning of any unknown words. These strategies will help children learn to analyze the text more thoroughly as they read.

When you are finished reading this book, turn to page 46 for **Text-Dependent Questions** a an **Extension Activity**.

TABLE of CONTENTS

IS IT A CRIME?

Crimes and punishments have been part of human civilization for thousands of years. In order for people to live among one another, there have to be rules for behavior—what the group finds acceptable versus what is a problem.

Motivations for crimes can vary widely. Need, jealousy, greed, hunger for power, and anger can all play a factor in someone's decision to commit a crime.

Sometimes people break laws for good reasons too. The "crimes" they commit are worth the consequences because they are trying to bring about positive changes. History has many examples of crimes that weren't really crimes and criminals who are seen as heroes today.

STICK 'EM UP!

STOPPED IN THEIR TRACKS

SAILES, LOUISIANA

There was little to do in the deep South during the Great Depression. People didn't have jobs or money. Many people were desperate. Some turned to crime to fill their time and their wallets, including the **notorious** crime-spree duo Bonnie and Clyde. Together, they robbed gas stations and country stores, stole cars, kidnapped people, and committed murder.

In 1934, Bonnie, 19, and Clyde, 21, helped five inmates escape from a prison in Waldo, Texas. This was the beginning of the end for them. FBI agents heard that the criminal couple was coming to Sailes, Louisiana, and they laid in wait. When Bonnie and Clyde drove through, they were gunned down and killed. Their partnership lasted only four years, but their legend is still alive today.

WARREN BEATTY
FAYE DUNAWAY

BROWNS

BONNIE AND CLYDE

FACT OR FICTION?

In 1967, a movie about Bonnie and Clyde was released starring two glamorous actors. According to biographer Jeff Guinn, the movie was about 95% fictional. The real Bonnie and Clyde were poor, Depression-era Texans. They rarely robbed banks because they weren't organized enough. Small country stores and gas stations were more their type.

ROBBING THE DUNBAR

LOS ANGELES, CALIFORNIA

In 1997, among the glitz and glamour of Los Angeles, California, five men pulled off one of the largest cash robberies in history. Allen Pace III worked at the Dunbar Armored Co. as a safety officer. Pace was fired but held on to his keys, which is how he and four **accomplices** entered the depot the next day.

In order to have an **alibi**, the men attended a party early in the evening. Then, around midnight, they broke into the Dunbar facility and loaded bags of cash into a rented moving van. In all, they stole $18.9 million, mostly in twenties. A broken piece of taillight found at the crime scene led to their capture.

AHOY, MATEYS!

You may picture pirates as movie or storybook characters of the past. In fact, pirates are alive and well today. Modern pirates use high-tech tools, like night-vision goggles, to zero in on their targets at sea. And like the pirates of old, they steal, plunder, and sometimes maroon their victims.

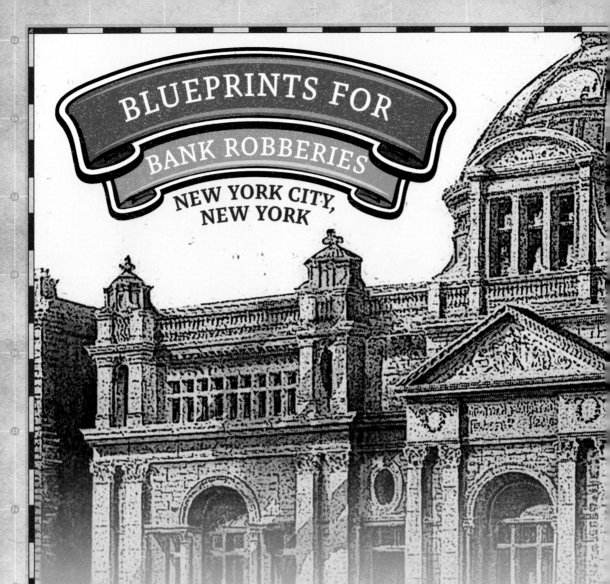

BLUEPRINTS FOR BANK ROBBERIES

NEW YORK CITY, NEW YORK

Post-Civil War New York City was crawling with desperate people looking for work. It was also home to a handful of wealthy business people and bank owners that architect, and soon-to-be bank robber, George Leslie Leonidas set his sights on.

Leslie snuck into fancy parties. As an architect, he asked wealthy bank owners questions about their banks and vaults. From this he created blueprints and **replicas** of banks and vaults for his hired bank-robbing gang to practice on.

New York City wasn't his only target. From 1869 until 1878, Leslie orchestrated about 80% of all bank robberies in the entire United States! But the problem with working with criminals is that they aren't the most trustworthy people. In 1878, George Leslie was murdered. The killer was never caught, but one of Leslie's accomplices was thought to be responsible.

SPY GUYS (AND GALS)

CONSPIRING WITH CUBA

WASHINGTON, DC

The mission of the American Defense Intelligence Agency (DIA) in Washington, DC, is to keep the United States safe. It hires people who want to protect and serve their country. But it turns out that Ana Montes, an employee in the 1980s, was not one of those people. In secret, she was committing acts of **treason**.

In 1984, Cuban president Fidel Castro recruited Montes as a spy. She didn't seek out this opportunity, but the role suited her, so she took it. For seventeen years, Montes passed along files and secrets to Communist Cuba while also excelling at her job in the DIA. Eventually, the FBI followed a lead that alerted them to her activities, and they arrested her.

In early 2023, Montes was released from prison after serving most of her sentence. Surprisingly, she has never shown remorse for her crimes.

ANA BELEN MONTES

DOB 02-28-57

WIRETAPPING IN THE WATERGATE BUILDING

WASHINGTON, DC

The Watergate Complex was built in Washington, DC, along the banks of the Potomac River. The modern buildings, landscaping, fountains, and views gave the business complex the feel of being its own town in the middle of a bustling city. It was here that five men were arrested for breaking into the Democratic National Committee (DNC) headquarters on June 17, 1972.

The men had been **wiretapping** the office to learn about the Democrats' strategy for the upcoming election. President Nixon's office denied any knowledge of the events, and he was reelected president in November 1972.

Two young reporters, Bob Woodward and Carl Bernstein, believed there was more to investigate. Information from an anonymous source confirmed their suspicions. Nixon was ordered to turn over tapes of conversations that he had at the White House. They revealed he was involved in the cover-up. Rather than being impeached, Nixon chose to resign—the only president to ever do so.

THE INVESTIGATION BEGINS

Frank Wills was the guard on duty when the Watergate break-in occurred. He noticed that the locks on several doors had been taped so they wouldn't lock. Thinking the cleaning crew had done this, he removed the tape. When he came back later, the tape was in place again. Wills called the police, which set the whole Watergate investigation in motion.

NATIONAL SECURITY SCANDAL

WASHINGTON, DC

The National Security Council (NSC) was created in 1947 to advise the president on domestic and foreign security issues. During the 1980s, Colonel Oliver North worked for the NSC under President Reagan. North was a supporter of the Nicaraguan Contras, a rebel group in Central America. This group used violent means to oppose the ruling dictator of Nicaragua. North raised money for the group by selling weapons to Iran. This scandal became known as the Iran-Contra Affair, and it led to Reagan firing North in 1985.

North went to trial and was accused of defrauding the government, obstructing Congress, and destroying documents. Although North lost his job and had to resign from the marines, he didn't go to prison. He was given just two years' probation.

CRIME IS OUR BUSINESS

CRIME BOSSES IN CHICAGO

CHICAGO, ILLINOIS

Chicago, Illinois, was a city that had been newly rebuilt in the 1920s after the devastating Great Fire of 1871. It was home to flappers, jazz clubs and musicians, immigrant neighborhoods, and a hopping nightlife. It was also home to a group of notorious gangsters—organized criminals known as the Mob or the Mafia.

You may have heard of some of the more famous members, such as Al Capone, John Dillinger, or John Gotti. Many mobsters were Italian immigrants, and they formed a crime network that snaked throughout the city.

ALCATRAZ ESCAPE

Alcatraz Island is located in California's San Francisco Bay. This "inescapable" prison housed some of America's most dangerous convicts. In 1962, three prisoners tunneled out of their cells through the vents. The chilly, rough waters could be deadly, so they made a raft out of stolen raincoats. The three men were never seen again. Was their escape successful?

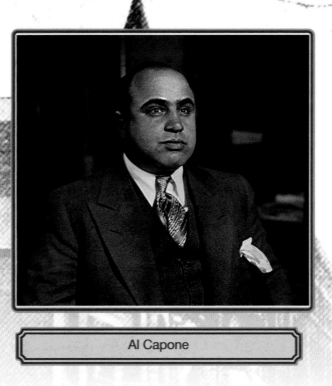

Al Capone

In 1920, Prohibition made it illegal to make or sell alcoholic beverages across the United States. But people continued making, selling, and transporting alcohol illegally (called bootlegging). Bootlegging and gambling were common Mafia activities. The Mob was also known for blackmail and **extortion**. Mobsters would demand that local businesses pay them regular fees. If they didn't pay up, mobsters would threaten the business owners with violence and even death.

Although gangsters were often arrested and imprisoned, there was always someone in "the Family" who could keep business rolling. And when one boss was killed or sent away, it meant that someone else was promoted—which often led to betrayals within the organization.

John Dillinger

George "Machine Gun" Kelly

George "Bugs" Moran

Don Vito Cascioferro, or Don Vito

KIDNAPPED IN CALIFORNIA

BERKELEY, CALIFORNIA

Berkeley, California, was a place of social change in the 1970s. The hippie movement of the 1960s was still widespread in Berkeley, which had been a hotbed of student protests. When Patty Hearst, a 19-year-old college student from a wealthy family, was kidnapped in 1974, Americans were captivated. Her kidnappers, a group of **domestic terrorists** called the Symbionese Liberation Army (SLA), demanded millions of dollars in food donations as ransom.

Although the SLA's demands were met, they didn't release Hearst. In fact, she allegedly became a willing member of the group—although she claimed to have been brainwashed. Hearst was seen on surveillance tapes helping to rob a bank. What started out as a kidnapping ended with the victim in jail for robbery!

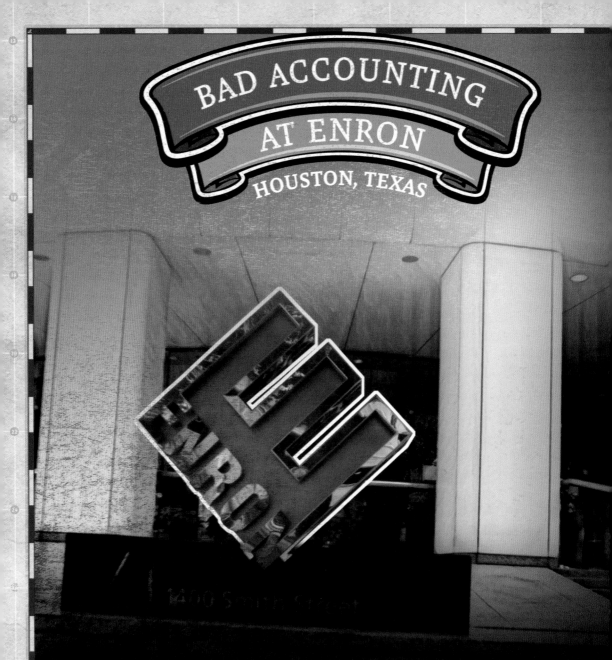

BAD ACCOUNTING AT ENRON

HOUSTON, TEXAS

The city of Houston, Texas, boasts one of the tallest skylines in North America. This booming city is known for its southern hospitality, diverse cultures, energy industry, and world-class dining and shopping. After 2001, Houston also became known for its association with the Enron scandal.

The 2001 Enron scandal is an example of a white-collar crime. The term *white collar* is usually used for people whose jobs don't require physical labor. They might work for a bank or a corporation instead. White-collar crimes tend to involve fraud, **embezzling** money, and tax evasion. People aren't usually physically hurt, but lives and businesses can be impacted or even destroyed.

When Enron's corruption and accounting fraud were made public, the Houston-based company went bankrupt. The price of one share of stock in the company went from about $90 to less than $1. Shareholders lost nearly all their money. Thousands of people lost their jobs in one of the largest American bankruptcies in history.

HIGH-TECH CRIME

The use of ransomware is a high-tech crime that businesses and individuals struggle to combat. Ransomware is a type of software that encrypts files. People must pay a ransom to unlock and access their own files. Technology is constantly evolving, but so are the criminals who use it!

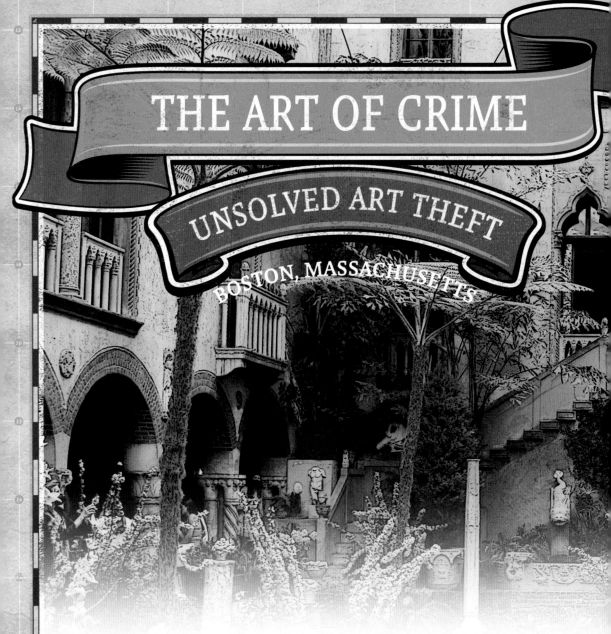

THE ART OF CRIME

UNSOLVED ART THEFT

BOSTON, MASSACHUSETTS

The Isabella Stewart Gardner Museum is located near Back Bay Fens, an urban park in a saltwater marshland in Boston, Massachusetts. It was the site of the biggest art **heist** in United States history, which is still an unsolved crime. If you can solve it, you might get a $10 million reward! In 1990, two men disguised as policemen entered the Gardner Museum. They tied up the security guards and stole 13 priceless works of art.

The thieves stole pieces by well-known artists, including Rembrandt, Vermeer, Degas, and Manet. In today's dollars, these artworks are worth $500 million! Empty frames still hang in the museum, waiting for the return of their occupants.

THE GREAT PRETENDER

*Is it a crime to pretend to be someone else? It depends on the situation. Ferdinand Demara was an **impostor** for most of his life, beginning when he took another man's name while in the army. His most notable impersonation was that of a surgeon on a ship during the Korean War. He operated on 16 casualties without killing anyone!*

FORGERY IN CALIFORNIA

LOS ANGELES, CALIFORNIA

Los Angeles had an exciting art scene in the 1970s and '80s. Galleries and art spaces were springing up, and people from all walks of life were coming together to make and exhibit art. It was the perfect environment for Tony Tetro, once the most famous art **forger** in America.

Tetro copied well-known artwork for fun. He read a book about an art forger and decided to try his hand at forgery. He fooled collectors, gallery owners, and museums with his talent and attention to detail . . . until he got caught. Tetro spent nine months in jail. Unlike most criminals, Tetro resumed doing what he loved—but in a legal way. Today, Tetro makes a good living selling his copies of Chagall, Picasso, and Dali paintings to knowing buyers.

WHAT A CRIME!

Most stolen artist: Pablo Picasso (more than 1,100 pieces of his artwork have been stolen)

Most famous stolen piece: Mona Lisa *by Leonardo da Vinci*

Most stolen piece: Ghent Altarpiece *by Jan van Eyck (stolen six times)*

Most valuable stolen piece: The Concert *by Johannes Vermeer (still missing; worth at least $250 million)*

WHEN A CRIME ISN'T A CRIME

SUFFRAGIST PROTEST
WASHINGTON, DC

The White House is located at 1600 Pennsylvania Avenue in the heart of Washington, DC, just over a mile from the Capitol Building. In January 1917, a group of female suffragists, called the Silent Sentinels, began picketing outside the White House. They were resolved to get President Wilson to support a federal amendment granting women the right to vote. But by June, the police were arresting women protesters.

THE ACCUSED

During the Salem witch trials of Massachusetts, about 200 people, mostly women, were accused of being witches. Twenty were put to death. They were seen as having unexplained "fits" (believed to be possession by the devil), or not fitting in with society. Paranoia, extreme religious beliefs, and no tolerance for differences meant that these innocent people were punished for committing no crime at all.

On November 14, 33 women were arrested and jailed in an event known as the Night of Terror. The conditions in the jail were filthy, the women were given wormy food, and they were physically abused.

By the beginning of 1918, it was ruled that the women had been imprisoned illegally. President Wilson began taking steps to actively support women's suffrage. Finally, by mid-1919, the Nineteenth Amendment passed, and women were allowed to vote. The suffragists saw that progress had resulted from their efforts. Imagine how proud they would have been to see Kamala Harris elected the first female vice president in 2020!

WE DEMAND
THAT THE
AMERICAN GOVERNMENT GIVE
ALICE PAUL
A POLITICAL OFFENDER.
THE PRIVILEGES RUSSIA GAVE MIYUNOFF

FIGHTING FOR EQUALITY

The 19th Amendment was not the end of the story when it came to voting rights for women. Due to continued discrimination against Black people, Native Americans, immigrants, and others, it would take many more years of fighting for all women to have voting rights. Many Black suffragettes, like Nannie Helen Burroughs, played a tremendous role in securing votes for women, however they were often left out of events and history books.

SK FREEDOM
WOMEN IS NOT
A CRIME

AGE PRISONERS
NOT BE TREATED
S CRIMINALS

MARCHING IN SELMA

SELMA, ALABAMA

Selma is a small city located near central Alabama, about 50 miles east of Montgomery, the capital. Although about half the city's population in the 1960s was Black, very few Black people were able to vote because of racist restrictions.

John Lewis, a civil rights activist, supported what he called "good trouble"—the idea that getting in trouble to make positive change is sometimes necessary (also known as civil disobedience). During Lewis's civil rights protests, he was arrested 40 times!

On March 7, 1965, Lewis tried to march from Selma to Montgomery. The protestors were peacefully marching for civil and voting rights when they were beaten and sprayed with tear gas by state troopers. The infamous day became known as Bloody Sunday. In August, the Voting Rights Act of 1965 was passed. John Lewis's "good trouble" meant that those restrictions keeping Black people, especially those in the South, away from voting polls were gone.

The 1940s and early '50s were a time of paranoia about the threat of Communism in the United States. It is referred to as the "Red Scare" because Communists were loyal to the Soviet Union, whose flag was red. Senator Joseph McCarthy led investigations into what he claimed was Communist activity in American institutions, including the White House, the army, and Hollywood. His accusations, however, weren't factual. McCarthy targeted people who didn't agree with his political views. He held enough power that these charges could be damaging to the lives, jobs, and reputations of those he accused.

Intellectuals and actors were popular targets for McCarthy. No one wanted to hire people who appeared on Hollywood blacklists for fear that they would be seen as supporting known Communists. The accused were expected to testify about their "un-American" activities and to turn in others (even if they didn't know any Communist supporters).

One of the most frightening parts about this time in history is how it compromised American freedoms—the right to free speech, to protest, and to join any political party.

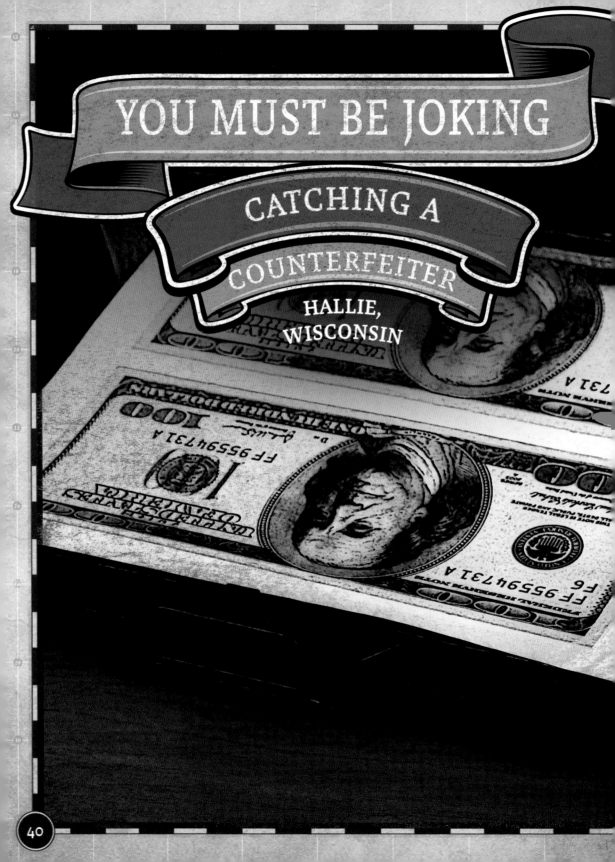

YOU MUST BE JOKING

CATCHING A COUNTERFEITER

HALLIE, WISCONSIN

Lake Hallie, a quiet village in Wisconsin, measures just under 15 square miles and borders a lake of the same name. Resident Jared Carr ran into some trouble one day when he visited a large retail store with a printer he wanted to return without a receipt. He had left a sheet of paper in the printer, and it had two $100 counterfeit bills printed on it!

Carr argued with the employees and refused to leave. They called the police, who found several more counterfeit bills in Carr's possession. It turned out that there was already an arrest warrant issued for him for previous crimes he had committed.

TINY TIGER

- - - - - - - - - - - - - - - - - -

Incidents of dognappings have been on the rise. One dognapper tried to disguise the Chihuahua he snatched by painting tiger stripes on it with hair dye! Police aren't sure what breed he was trying to imitate, but Baby Cakes was safely returned to her owner—and luckily the stripes weren't permanent.

- - - - - - - - - - - - - - - - - -

Over the years, Grapevine, Texas, has been known for producing cotton, cantaloupes, and, of course, grapes. It also produced a bumbling criminal—a man who was arrested by a police officer while trying to impersonate one. He didn't have a police car, but he outfitted his white pickup truck with lights similar to undercover police cars.

The faux officer didn't give quite as much attention to his badge though. He made a police "badge" out of a Mexican restaurant gift card and didn't bother to cover up the name of the chain restaurant on it. If he pulled someone over, they wouldn't know if they were getting a ticket or a taco!

LAWS YOU AREN'T LIKELY TO BREAK

- *In Washington, killing Bigfoot is a felony.*

- *In Tennessee, you can't hold public office if you've been in a duel.*

- *At one point, it was illegal to put ice cream on cherry pie in Kansas!*

- *It's illegal to drive blindfolded in Alabama. (Does this mean it's legal in other states?)*

WE TRAVELED TO...

Find the location of each place you've traveled to while reading this book.

1. **Waldo, Texas**

2. **Sailes, Louisiana**

3. **Los Angeles, California**

4. **Washington, DC**

5. **New York City, New York**

6. **Chicago, Illinois**

7. **San Francisco Bay (Alcatraz Island)**

8. **Berkeley, California**

9. **Houston, Texas**

10. **Boston, Massachusetts**

11. **Salem, Massachusetts**

12. **Selma, Alabama**

13. **Lake Hallie, Wisconsin**

14. **Hollywood, California**

15. **Grapevine, Texas**

GLOSSARY

accomplices (uh-KAHM-plis-ehz): people who help other people commit crimes

alibi (AL-uh-bye): a defense in which one claims to have been elsewhere at the time a crime occurred

domestic terrorists (duh-MES-tik TER-ur-ists): people who commit violent, criminal acts against others in the same country

embezzling (em-BEZ-uhl-ing): secretly stealing money from the place you work for

extortion (ik-STORE-shuhn): the act of using threats or force to make someone give up something valuable, like money or information

heist (highst): a hold-up or armed robbery

forger (FOR-jer): a person who makes a copy of something

impostor (im-PAH-stur): a person who poses as someone else

notorious (no-TOR-ee-uhs): widely and unfavorably known

replicas (REP-li-kuhz): exact copies of things, sometimes on a smaller scale than the original

treason (TREE-zuhn): the crime of being disloyal to your country by giving information to its enemies or acting against it in some way

wiretapping (WYE-ur tap-ing): attaching a concealed device, usually to a telephone, in order to obtain information

INDEX

TEXT-DEPENDENT QUESTIONS

1. Who were the Silent Sentinels?

2. Why did President Nixon resign?

3. Why do you think the Mafia is known as a type of organized crime?

4. How were the Salem witch trials and McCarthyism similar?

5. In what way did George Leslie Leonidas lead a double life?

EXTENSION ACTIVITY

You've learned about all sorts of crimes. But what about the people who solve them? Forensic scientists are key in the quest to make sense of the evidence found at crime scenes. They analyze DNA, fingerprints, handwriting, weapons, tools, and all sorts of other evidence to lead them to the culprit and a solution to the mystery. If you'd like to try your hand at using forensic science, search "PBS DNA fingerprint" online for a fun activity.

BIBLIOGRAPHY

"Chicago Outfit." *American Mafia History*, https://americanmafiahistory.com/chicago-outfit/. Accessed October 25, 2022.

Art Market, https://artmarketmag.com/tony-tetro-an-interview-with-genius-art-forger/. Accessed October 21, 2022.

"Bonnie and Clyde." *FBI*, https://www.fbi.gov/history/famous-cases/bonnie-and-clyde. Accessed October 18, 2022.

"McCarthyism and the Red Scare." *Miller Center*, https://millercenter.org/the-presidency/educational-resources/age-of-eisenhower/mcarthyism-red-scare. Accessed October 26, 2022.

Popkin, Jim. "Ana Montes did much harm spying for Cuba. Chances are, you haven't heard of her," *The Washington Post*, April 18, 2013. https://www.washingtonpost.com/sf/feature/wp/2013/04/18/ana-montes-did-much-harm-spying-for-cuba-chances-are-you-havent-heard-of-her/.

"The June 1962 Alcatraz Escape." *PBS*, https://www.pbs.org/wnet/secrets/alcatraz-escape-june-1962-alcatraz-escape/2667/. Accessed October 25, 2022.

McGreevy, Nora. "What to Know About the Gardner Museum Heist." *Smithsonian Magazine*, April 9, 2021, https://www.smithsonianmag.com/smart-news/five-things-know-about-isabella-stewart-gardner-art-heist-180977448/. Accessed October 21, 2022.

Tracy, Kathleen. *The Watergate Scandal*. Mitchell Lane Publishers, 2007.

Lisa Kurkov is a freelance writer and editor who lives in North Carolina with her husband, two children, and a variety of animals. When her head isn't buried in a book, Lisa enjoys baking, crafting, photography, birding, and adventuring with her family. She enjoys reading the occasional crime thriller but does her best to steer clear of real-life crime scenes.

www.rourkebooks.com

PHOTO CREDITS ©: Cover: Andrey_Kuzmin/ Shutterstock.com; Cover: Jennifer_Sharp/ Getty Images; Cover: Marco Rubino/ Shutterstock.com; Cover: Diego Grandi/ Shutterstock.com; Cover: michaeljung/ Getty Images; Page 1: MrsWilkins/ Getty Images; Page 1 ricorico/ Getty Images; Page 1: prochasson frederic/ Shutterstock.com; Page 1: EVA CARRE/ Shutterstock.com; Page 1: happiness time/ Shutterstock.com; Page 4-5: EVA CARRE/ Shutterstock.com; Page 5: happiness time/ Shutterstock.com; Page 6-7: Polaris/Newscom; Page 7: WARNER BROTHERS/ Album/ Newscom; Page 8: Jezper/ Shutterstock.com; Page 8-9: anushkaniroshan/ Shutterstock.com: Page 9: Nick Jio/ Unsplash; Page 10-11: Internet Archive Book Images/ Wikimedia Commons; Page 11: Heritage Auctions/ Wikimedia Commons; Page 12-13: alexskopje/ Shutterstock.com; Page 13: Federal Bureau of Investigation/ Wikimedia Commons; Page 14: akg-images/ Newscom; Page 14-15: akg-images/ Newscom; Page 15: ASSOCIATED PRESS; Page 16-17: Ron Sachs/ ZUMA Press/ Newscom; Page 18-19: Everett Collection/ Newscom; Page 19: kyolshin/ Newscom; Page 20: Jecinci/ Mediadrumworld.Com/ ZUMA Press/ Newscom; Page 20-21: Internet Archive Book Images/ Wikimedia Commons; Page 21: Jecinci/ Mediadrumworld. Com/ ZUMA Press/ Newscom; Page 21: Everett Collection/Newscom; Page 21: Jecinci/ Mediadrumworld.Com/ ZUMA Press/ Newscom; Page 21: Jecinci/ Mediadrumworld.Com/ ZUMA Press/ Newscom; Page 22: Everett Collection/Newscom; Page 23: Everett Collection/Newscom; Page 24-25: James Nielson/ ZUMAPRESS/ Newscom; Page 25: James Nielson/ ZUMAPRESS/ Newscom; Page 25: rawf8/ Shutterstock.com; Page 26-27: Jennifer Shishmanian/ Unsplash; Page 27: Associated Newspapers/ Rex Features/ Wikimedia Commons; Page 28-29: Natali Brillianata/ Shutterstock.com; Page 29: Steve Taylor/ SOPA Images/ Sipa USA/ Newscom; Page 30-31: Harris & Ewing/ Heritage Art/ Heritage Images AiWire/ Newscom; Page 31: JT Vintage/ Glasshouse Images/ Newscom; Page 32-33: Glasshouse Images /Glasshouse Images/ Newscom; Page 33: Circa Images/Newscom; Page 34-35: ASSOCIATED PRESS; Page 36-37: Everett Collection/ Newscom; Page 38-39: Everett Collection/ Newscom; Page 39: World History Archive/ Newscom; Page 40-41: Africa Studio/ Shutterstock.com; Page 41: Lesia Kapinosova/Shutterstock.com; Page 42-43: badmanproduction/ Getty Images; Page 42-43: Nerthuz; Page 42-43: Rawpixel; Page 42-43: Happy_vector; Page 42-43: Elizabeth Lara; Page 42-43: Vac1; Page various: LoudRedCreative/ Getty Images; Page various: Anna Timoshenko/ Shutterstock.com; Page various: Miodrag Kitanovic/ Getty Images; Page various: Andrey_Kuzmin/ Shutterstock.com

Library of Congress PCN Data

The Scene of the Crime / Lisa Kurkov

(Travel to...)

ISBN 978-1-73165-731-2 (hard cover)

ISBN 978-1-73165-718-3 (soft cover)

ISBN 978-1-73165-744-2 (e-book)

ISBN 978-1-73165-757-2 (e-pub)

Library of Congress Control Number: 2023942376

Rourke Educational Media

Printed in the United States of America

01-2722311937

Edited by: **Catherine Malaski**

Cover and interior design/illustration by: **Max Porter**